Cambridge English

Level 5

Series editor: Philip Prowse

A Tangled Web

Alan Maley

CAMBRIDGE
UNIVERSITY PRESS

CAMBRIDGE
UNIVERSITY PRESS

University Printing House, Cambridge CB2 8BS, United Kingdom

Cambridge University Press is part of the University of Cambridge.

It furthers the University's mission by disseminating knowledge in the pursuit of education, learning and research at the highest international levels of excellence.

www.cambridge.org
Information on this title: www.cambridge.org/9780521536646

First published 2004
Reprinted 2016

Printed in the United Kingdom by Hobbs the Printers Ltd

A catalogue record for this publication is available from the British Library

ISBN 978-0-521-53664-6 Paperback

For Nanny, Joris, Paul, Jeanne, Camille et Julie

Contents

Characters

Dan Combes: a former MI6 agent
Annie Combes: Dan's daughter
Jurgen Heid, **Nina Rowlandson**, **Cas Cousins:** former
   MI6 agents
Bert Perkins: an old colleague of Dan's at MI6
Hugo Strang: an MI6 director
Sir Clive Horley: a senior MI6 director
Sir George: Dan's former boss

> Oh, what a tangled web we weave,
> When first we practise to deceive!
> Sir Walter Scott, *Marmion*

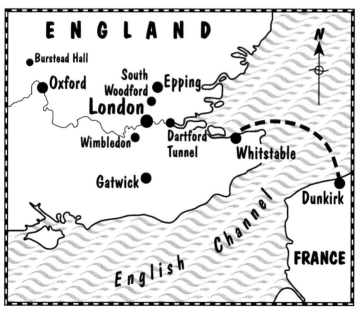

The Valley

It is a late afternoon in September. The scene is a valley in south-western France. The river flows slowly between the steep, wooded hills. The sun is shining on the water. It is quiet. A man is sitting on a flat rock, which sticks out into the river. He is alone. He sits absolutely still. Like a stone statue. After a while he bends to look at something in the water – a fish perhaps. As he does so, something hits the water and there is a sudden splash. He puts his hand to his ear. It is covered with blood. He falls forward into the river and disappears into its muddy water.

Chapter 1 *The River*

The pain exploded in my ear sending shockwaves through my body. When I saw the blood on my hand, I knew it was a bullet. Someone had shot at me from the hillside. I immediately fell forward, and swam underwater further up the river. Far above me the green and yellow light of the surface seemed out of reach. But I had to swim as far upriver as I could. They might fire at me again if I showed my head above the surface. When I felt as if I could swim no further, I came up under some trees by the river bank. Here I was safe. No one could see me from the hillside.

My heart was racing. Someone had tried to kill me. Why would anyone want to kill me? Where were they now? What would they do next?

I forced myself to be calm. All my old spy training came back to me: stop and think before you act; decide on the most important thing to do; take one thing at a time. Above all, never panic, never lose your cool, always stay calm.

Whoever had shot at me would probably come to check that I was dead. I decided to find a place to hide and wait there. Slowly and carefully, I crept on hands and knees along the river bank until I could see the rock clearly again. I sat down behind some bushes, and waited. I pressed my wet shirt against my ear to try and stop the bleeding. Only five minutes later I heard the sound of someone coming down the path from the hillside.

He was a tall man about my age. He had his back to me, so I could not see his face. But when he looked in my direction, I saw that it was . . . Heid! He turned and walked down the path.

Chapter 2 *On the Hillside*

Two hundred metres up on the hillside a man and a woman were arguing. Through the branches of the trees they had a clear view of the rock in the river. They spoke in whispers so no one would hear them. But they were very tense and angry. The man was still holding the rifle he had just fired.

'What happened? Did you get him?' the woman asked.

'I'm not sure. He moved just as I fired. But he fell into the river, so I think I got him.'

'You think!' whispered the woman fiercely. 'Thinking is not good enough. We have to be sure. We have to find the body. To be sure he's dead.'

'OK, OK. Don't let's waste any more time. I'll go down to the rock. If I can't find him there, I'll look further up the river. You'd better take the path down towards the bridge. It's possible his body has been carried down by the current of the river. But the river is flowing very slowly so it will take some time.'

'I'm not happy about splitting up. Maybe we should stay together. Suppose he isn't dead. You know how dangerous he is. I wouldn't want to meet him on my own.'

'Don't worry about it,' the man said. 'Here, take my pistol. But I'm pretty sure you won't need it. He must be dead.'

'All right. I just hope you're right. Where shall we meet?'

'Go to the café by the bridge if you don't find him. You know – the place where we left the car. I'll join you there.'

Chapter 3   *The Fight*

Jurgen Heid – a friend. Why had he tried to kill me? I didn't understand. We had been on the San Cristobal operation together: Heid, Nina, Cas and me. We were a team until the operation failed. We had all been sent to 'safe' houses after that. But we were not supposed to meet again – ever. We were all told to disappear, to start new lives, to become other people. Above all, we were told never to meet each other again. That was five years ago. So how had Heid found me? Someone must have sent him. But who? And why? What had happened to bring him here?

As I watched, Heid came back to the river bank. He put his rifle against a tree and took out a pair of binoculars. Slowly he looked along the other bank of the river. He was obviously looking for my body. I suddenly felt angry. He had been my friend, and he had tried to kill me. And now he was looking for my body. I had to find out why he had tried to kill me, and who had sent him.

I picked up a thick piece of wood lying near my hiding place. My ear was bleeding heavily but I tried to ignore the pain. Quietly and carefully, I crept up behind Heid. He was so busy looking at the river through his binoculars that he did not notice me. I brought the stick down hard on the back of his head. He fell down, and rolled a little further down the river bank. I thought I had knocked him out but, as I bent over him, he suddenly grabbed me. I felt his hands around my throat, slowly squeezing the breath out of me. The stick was still in my hand and with the last of my energy I brought it down on his head. He let go of my throat immediately. In a sudden burst of anger, I began to hit him again and again with the stick. As my anger left me, I realised that I had gone too far. Heid was dead. I had foolishly lost my chance to find the answers to my questions. And all because of my anger.

Heid's body was now at the bottom of the river bank. His face was in the water – and the slow current of the river carried away a steady flow of blood. I pulled the body along the river bank, to a place where some overhanging trees and low bushes hid me from any curious eyes. I need not have worried. It was evening, and I knew that anyone out fishing or hiking would already be going home. The surface of the river was still, except for the occasional fish jumping for flies. Far away a church clock struck seven. It was a perfect autumn evening.

First I had to hide the body. Then I had to find out if it was safe to return to the house. After this attack, it would not be safe for me to stay in the village – but where should I go? And then I had to find out why Heid had come after me, and who had sent him.

In the pocket of his shorts there was a set of car keys – with a registration number on the key ring. I put the keys in my pocket. There was only one place where Heid could have parked a car – outside the café. It might be useful later.

I rolled the body into the water, pushed it into a hole under the river bank, and put some large stones on top of it to hold it under the water. I picked up Heid's rifle, and then set off for the village. It was almost dark by the time I reached the house.

Chapter 4   *The House*

I had chosen the house for its position. It stood on the corner of the steep road which led up into the village of Sauvelagarde, just outside the village itself. Behind the house there was a steep rock face; the village itself was on the top. I had a view of the whole valley in both directions. No one could approach the village without being seen. And no one could reach the house from behind. It was perfect. And – something which only I knew – there was a small entrance to the house from below the road. I had put in a steel door which led along a tunnel under the road and into my cellar, and from there into the house above. I checked that no one was around, then pressed the combination on the lock, and made my way along the tunnel into the dark of the cellar.

I always left a torch in the cellar and once I had found it, I waited in silence for a moment. I knew that if there was anything unusual in the house, I would know. I had a kind of sixth sense that always warned me of danger. It had often saved my life in the past. Above me, the house creaked, but the sound was not unusual – just an old house settling down for the night. I could hear bats flying around in the darkness of the cellar. That too was normal. Everything felt normal; I felt sure that there was no one in the house. I placed Heid's rifle carefully against the wall.

I unlocked the door into the house. I didn't switch on the lights. No one from the village must know I was still around. I stuck some bandage over my ear to try and stop the bleeding. Then I quickly packed an overnight bag and changed into clean, dry clothes. Lastly, I took the picture off the wall and unlocked the big steel safe hidden behind it.

I took out my automatic pistol, some money, my passport and the brown envelope containing the CDs. I was just about to put everything into my briefcase, when I heard footsteps coming towards the front door. I quickly switched off the torchlight, put everything into the kitchen table drawer out of sight, and stood completely still. The footsteps stopped at the front door.

'Hello!' said a voice. 'Monsieur Daniel? Monsieur Daniel? Anyone home?'

I recognised the voice as an old man from the village. I kept quite still. After what seemed an age, I heard his footsteps returning to the village above. I switched the torch back on but the light died almost immediately. Damn! I opened the drawer in the dark and hurriedly put my things into the briefcase.

I felt my way like a blind man back down the stairs into the cellar, through the tunnel and out of the house. The sky was still glowing pink with the memory of the day, and I could see the dark shape of the church at the top of the hill. From the village above came the familiar sounds of people talking over supper.

I made my way soundlessly down towards the river, staying off the road. At the bridge I crouched down behind the wall until I was sure no one was around. Then I ran quickly across the bridge to the darkness of the car park next to the café. I stayed out of the pool of light coming from the café windows. I could see customers inside. I recognised two villagers drinking at the bar. They were regular customers. Nothing unusual there. But then I saw a woman sitting at a corner table in half-darkness. My heart almost stopped beating. It was Nina! I hadn't seen her for five years. She was still as beautiful as I remembered her. So Nina had come with Heid. Two of the old team had come to kill me – the third. She looked at her watch with a worried expression. She was obviously waiting for Heid. Suddenly, she looked up towards the windows. I immediately crouched down out of Nina's sight. She was a dangerous woman.

I walked over to the cars in the café car park. There were only three of them. I checked the registration plates against the keys I'd taken from Heid and quietly got into his car. Luckily it was parked at the top of the slope running down towards the bridge. I took off the brake and let it roll silently down the slope and on to the bridge. As it gathered speed, I started the engine, and drove down into the valley. A few hundred metres down the valley, I pulled off the road under some trees. I switched off the lights, got out of the car, and crouched down in the darkness among the trees. I waited for ten minutes. No cars passed. I could just see the lights of the café through the trees. There was no movement there. I got back into the car and drove away.

Chapter 5   *Hotel des Templiers*

I drove towards Toulouse. What was going on? I tried to sort out my thoughts again. Heid had come to kill me. He had not come alone; Nina had been with him. So two of the old team had worked together to kill me. It was unbelievable. My old colleagues. How had Nina and Heid found each other? And how had they found me? And, what was more important, why had they tried to murder me? Nina, Heid and Daniel: we were the only three left of the four. We had left Cas dead at Bambacocha. The only person who knew where we all were was Sir George, our former boss in London. But I could not believe he would be involved in something like this. Unless there was someone else. A memory suddenly flashed across my mind – two men deep in conversation in a dark Berlin office. I pushed it away, and concentrated on my driving. In the distance I could see the lights of a village on a hilltop. I checked the time – nine o'clock already. I tried to guess what they would expect me to do. By now Nina would have gone out to look for Heid, and discovered that the car was gone. She would have put two and two together and guessed that I had somehow escaped. She would have phoned someone to let them know. Where would that someone look for me? They would probably expect me to make for Toulouse and the airport. I decided not to do what they expected.

Halfway to Gaillac I turned off down a narrow country road towards Puycelsi. Half an hour later, I parked the car at the Hotel des Templiers in the old town. Luckily they had a room free. I checked in and suddenly realised how hungry I was. It was well past dinner time but the owner kindly made me a plate of country ham, sausage and goat cheese which tasted like food for the gods, especially when washed down with a bottle of the local red wine. Before going to bed, I walked round the narrow streets of the small town. Outside the post office I found a public pay phone and dialled a Toulouse number.

'Annie?'

'Yes. Is that you Dad? What's going on?'

'What do you mean?'

'Well, I haven't heard from you for ages. Then, this evening, someone called, I don't know who – a woman – asking if I've seen you. I nearly collapsed. I told her what you'd always told me to say. I said that you were dead, that you'd died five years ago. And now you call . . . What's going on, Dad?' Her voice was full of suspicion, 'What are you up to?'

'Annie, I'm sorry. I'll explain when I see you.'

'OK, Dad. But when will I see you? Where are you?'

'It's better I don't tell you now. Do one thing for me, though, will you? I'd like you to pick me up outside the supermarket in Castelnau tomorrow morning at nine thirty. Can you do that? In the meantime, don't tell anyone we've spoken and don't say where you're going tomorrow morning. We'd both be in danger if anyone found out. And bring an overnight bag. And don't forget that . . . ' The phone went dead; my coins had run out.

Chapter 6   *Meeting in Castelnau*

I parked the car in a narrow road behind the main street of Castelnau. Heid had hired the car at Toulouse airport and the hire papers, in the name of Baumann, were under the seat. I had a quick look at the papers. Heid had given an address in Schleswig-Holstein, Germany. There was also a telephone number. It might be worth trying later. I got out, and looked in the boot of the car. There was a small suitcase. It contained women's clothes. Poor Nina would have to do without clean clothes today! I locked the car and threw the keys into some bushes. If they found the car, they would have to break into it.

Castelnau is a red brick village, with a big red brick church, only twenty minutes from Toulouse. It was just small enough to make sure that we wouldn't miss each other, and just large enough for the meeting to attract no attention. I checked the time – nine fifteen. I had arrived early to check the meeting place, just in case Annie's phone had been tapped and they knew about our meeting. I ordered a coffee in a bar just across the road from the small supermarket. The man served me without speaking. He was a silent man with a cigarette hanging from his bottom lip. He spent his time rearranging the dirt on the bar counter with what looked like some of his wife's old underwear. I wondered uneasily what the man had used to filter the coffee.

There was nothing unusual across the road. One or two

old ladies entered and left the store, but no one was waiting around. At nine twenty-five Annie appeared, driving her old car, just as I remembered it. I paid for the coffee, leaving it still undrunk on the counter, ran across the road and got in quickly.

'Just drive towards Toulouse. We'll talk in a minute.'

The rush hour traffic was getting lighter now, so we were soon approaching the ring road round the city.

'How much time do you have?' I asked.

'I'm not working at the moment, so I'm free for the rest of the week. I need to be back by Friday, though. I've got to take Lucien to see his mother in hospital. You never said, but I guessed you might need the car for some time.'

'Lucien? Oh yes, the one I met last time. The one with purple hair.' I smiled. 'Are you two still together then?'

'Dad. You know that I don't allow questions like that! I live my life the way I want. OK?'

'All right, all right, Annie. Forget I asked.'

'OK. Just don't do it again. All right? Now, where are we going?'

She bit her lip nervously, and suddenly I remembered her as a little girl again. It was something she used to do whenever she was really unhappy or worried about something. I decided it was better not to ask any more questions.

'Can you take the motorway to Barcelona? We can be there by this afternoon. You can stay overnight and come back tomorrow morning. Have you got your passport?'

'Yes, Dad. And my overnight bag. Remember what you taught me? Be prepared! You certainly prepared me to look after myself.' She smiled a bitter smile.

'OK, OK. I know. I was a terrible father. Please don't remind me!'

'Dad, you weren't a terrible father . . . just a bit – unusual, let's say. But I've had a really bad time dealing with your secrecy. All those times you arrived in the middle of the night and then just disappeared again. All those strange phone calls. I wish you could try to trust me a bit more.'

'I'm sorry, Annie, but it's too dangerous for you if I tell you everything.'

'Well, can't you explain what happened last night at least?'

She reached for a cigarette and lit it with one hand. With the other hand, she guided the car at 100 kph around the ring road, moving in and out of the morning traffic.

'Slow down a bit, Annie. You're making me nervous with your driving. I don't want to get killed now after all I've been through . . . And I don't want to die of cancer from your cigarette smoke, either.'

'Mind your own business, Dad. If you ride in my car, you have to put up with the driver's habits. If you don't like them, you know what you can do. OK?'

Chapter 7 *Journey to Barcelona*

'All right. I'll tell you what I can – what it's safe for you to know, OK?'

She nodded, 'That should help to pass the time! And maybe it'll take your mind off my driving.'

'OK. Five years ago I was involved in a special operation in Central America. The Americans, the CIA, wanted someone to do their dirty work for them, so they called MI6 in London. One of our MI6 directors saw his chance for promotion, so he dreamed up this plan. The president of this Central American country was someone the Americans had supported. He was very anti-terrorist and pro-capitalism. But he was also heavily involved in the drug business. The Americans looked the other way for years, but he started getting too greedy. He was becoming an embarrassment to the US government. Newspaper and television journalists back in Washington were starting to ask awkward questions. So the CIA decided to get rid of him. But – and here's the complication – as ever, there was a revolutionary group that opposed the President and his government. If anything happened to the President, they would've taken control. And the CIA didn't want this to happen. So four of us from MI6 were supposed to go in and give the revolutionaries support and training to take out the dictator. Then, we would leave and hand over everything we knew about them to the CIA. After that the CIA would knock out the revolutionaries, too. They would then arrange for "democratic" elections, and bring back an old-style politician to lead the new government. Win-win for the CIA, lots of praise for MI6, promotion for the director in London. Do you follow me?'

'Yes. But why couldn't the CIA do it themselves?'

'The political situation was too sensitive. If anyone had found out, there would have been big trouble back home – embarrassing questions in the House of Representatives, articles in the newspapers, all that kind of thing. And the new US President was concerned about the activities of the CIA at the time. It was easier to get us to do it.'

'So you went?'

'Right. Four of us. Our cover was that we were a group of independent soldiers or mercenaries. The revolutionaries were told that we were paid by an anti-capitalist organisation in Europe. We knew that if they ever found out the truth, we would be on our own. London would deny that we had anything to do with them. Washington would pretend they knew nothing. Everyone would turn their backs on us, and look the other way.'

'It sounds a bit risky to me. Why did you agree to do it?'

'You're right there,' I said. 'I should have smelt trouble before we even began.'

'So, there was trouble?'

'Oh yes. Plenty of trouble,' I went on. 'Everything went fine to begin with. We landed by boat at night, the revolutionaries met us, and we went with them. Then we spent three months in their camps, training them in weapons and explosives. We nearly got to the president, too – one of our team was a very attractive woman, and he loved attractive women. She was supposed to poison him during a performance at the opera! But that was when things started to go badly wrong.'

'What happened?'

'Someone obviously knew about our plan, and we were stopped on our way to the Opera House. Luckily, we were able to kill the soldiers who stopped us. We had a plan for this kind of emergency. We had all agreed to escape back into the jungle and meet up at a village called Bambacocha, near the Chichiguarani Falls. But government commandos were waiting for us. They caught one of us, our leader, and shot him. The other three of us got away. We spent a month hiding in the jungle. Eventually we got to the coast and found a boat to escape to Honduras. The British High Commissioner was very surprised to see us!'

'Then what happened?'

'When we got back to London it was obvious that we were an embarrassment to MI6. They kept us locked up in a big country house in Oxfordshire for what they called "debriefing". We were all questioned about what had happened. They were especially interested in what we had found out about the drug business in San Cristobal. I think they couldn't decide what to do with us. It would have been better for them if we had all died – then there would have been no problem. So they decided to make us disappear instead.'

'What do you mean?'

'They gave us new identities: new names, new passports, everything . . . We all got a generous amount of money to live on, and they sent us to different "safe" places to live for the rest of our lives. But we all had to sign up to special conditions. We had to agree never to contact each other again – no phone calls, postcards, nothing. We were told never to contact MI6 again, and never to tell anyone who we really were or what we'd done – especially the press. In a way, our new identity was a kind of prison. Anyway, I don't know where the others went. I kept my promise. I never tried to contact either of them, and I kept my mouth shut about what we'd done. This is the first time I have told anyone anything about that operation.'

'So, why are you here now, Dad? Why are we going to Barcelona?'

'Well, everything went well for five years, till yesterday. Then, two of my old team suddenly turned up – and tried to murder me.'

'Murder you? But why would they want to do that?'

'That's just what I've been wondering myself. In fact, it's made me wonder about a lot of things. I wonder if they intended us all to die in Bambacocha. Perhaps they wanted us to be killed. We had failed to kill the dictator, but we knew far too much.'

'You mean they would kill their own people?'

'Yes, of course. These people have no principles at all. It's all about power, politics – and money, of course.'

'But that doesn't explain why your old team came to kill you, does it? I mean, why were they trying to get rid of you? Anyway, what happened exactly?'

'Well, I was lucky. I'm still here. Though part of my ear isn't – as you can see. One of them wasn't so lucky. And I've no idea what the other one – the woman – is doing now. But I need to find out. And I'll have to go to London for that.'

'So why are we going to Barcelona? You could fly to London from Toulouse, couldn't you?'

'Of course I could. But I think that is just what "they" are expecting me to do. I don't want them to know where I am. Barcelona is better.'

'OK, Dad. If you say so.'

We stopped talking for a while. Soon afterwards the towers and mediaeval walls of Carcassonne appeared in the distance. It looked like Disneyland. The kilometres sped by and we were soon turning south, heading for Perpignan and the Spanish border.

'Isn't it strange the way these motorways have changed the way we think about things?'

'How do you mean, Dad?'

'Well, before motorways, roads were sort of natural – they grew out of the shape of the country. The shape of the roads fitted the shape of the valleys and hillsides. Motorways just cut holes through the countryside. If you want to get from A to B, you just draw a line on a map and then build a road through. So when we travel on these roads, we don't look at the landscape – or not in the same way as before. It's all speed. Everything has to be immediate, instant. Instant noodles, instant coffee . . . There's no time for quiet thinking or enjoyment. I remember driving down from Paris to the Mediterranean coast with your mother, over 30 years ago. It took us three whole days. Now you can do it in one.'

There was an uncomfortable silence.

'Dad . . . can I ask you something?

'Of course you can. What about?'

'Well, it's always bothered me, but I never found the

right time to ask you before . . . What exactly happened between you and Mum? Why did you split up? I could never understand . . .'

'It's difficult to explain. I suppose we reached the point where we disagreed about almost everything. She didn't like my lifestyle – all those unexplained absences, the long trips away from home. I had no real friends – friends didn't go with my kind of job! And I couldn't stand her friends. She wanted a life where everything was in its place, everything was certain, everything was safe and respectable: a nice house, a nice garden, a nice car, a nice husband wearing a nice suit and tie. She should have married a bank manager but she got me instead!'

'But you stayed together for so long Dad, nearly ten years.'

'I know. But you get into the habit of living with someone. So, in a way, it's more comfortable to continue with the habit than to break it. It's a mixture of being lazy and weak. The one day, you wake up, you look at this person who you thought you knew so well, and you simply can't recognise them any more. I think that's what happened.'

'I was so unhappy all that time we lived in Paris, Dad. There was always so much tension in the air. Then, after it was over, all those tears. I remember those weekends we spent together, you and me. You didn't really know how to pass the time. You tried so hard to make me enjoy myself. All those trips to cinemas in Paris, to places you thought I'd like – the Luxembourg gardens, the zoo . . . But that made it feel even worse. I couldn't wait to get back to Mum again. But then the moment I got back, I felt miserable with her, too. Because when I was with her, I missed you so much.'

'I wish I hadn't hurt you like that. You were the main reason I waited so long before . . . But in the end, I had to do it. There's no point in worrying about it now. It's past history. At least you learnt how to look after yourself, how to be independent.'

'Thanks for nothing!' she said, with a bitter grin.

The motorway climbs steeply into the Pyrenees towards the border. Luckily customs hardly bother to check cars these days. We are all Europeans now! They only do random checks, mainly on long-distance lorries. Annie was waved through, and we were suddenly in Spain, rolling down towards Barcelona.

*   *   *

We checked into a small hotel in the old town, and I left Annie to rest while I went to a travel agent. I was in luck. There were seats on a morning flight to London the next day. I paid cash. That evening, I took Annie to one of my favourite restaurants in the tangled web of narrow streets off the Ramblas. As we ate and talked, I think we both sensed that it might be a long time before we would enjoy each other's company like this again. But for the first time in years, I felt close to my daughter. It was a rare and special moment.

Chapter 8   *Bert Perkins*

I took a taxi to the airport early the next morning. I didn't want to risk anyone identifying Annie's car, so I left her at the hotel.

'I can't tell you exactly where I'm going,' I told her, 'but I will be in touch as soon as I can. Let's use email. And be nice to Lucien, OK? Oh, and drive carefully.' Then I left.

Airports are wonderfully anonymous places. No one knows who all the other people are. The crowds gather, mix together, then go off through the departure gates to the four corners of the world. As they leave, new groups of tired or excited travellers arrive. But airports are also dangerous places, especially if you are a 'wanted' person. Those video cameras are everywhere – eyes that never close for sleep. And there are those apparently ordinary men – so ordinary that no one notices them. Men who sit for long hours, checking the crowds pretending to read their newspapers. Occasionally one of them will take out a mobile phone and make a call. On the other side of the airport, another man will reply. Sometimes police will then appear and lead away an ordinary-looking passenger.

This was the trap that I had to escape from. It was a risk. I still wasn't sure if I'd been followed. I felt the palms of my hands grow sweaty as I approached the check-in desk, but I needn't have worried. I passed through without a problem.

The flight was called soon afterwards. It wasn't full, and I had a window seat in a row by myself. I thought back over the events of the past two days, trying to make sense of the attack at the river. How had they got together, Nina and Heid? And how had they found me? My mind wandered as I thought about all the parallel lives going on at this moment below me. I imagined Annie, starting the long drive back to her lover in Toulouse. I thought of Nina. Where would she be now? I thought of Hugo Strang, the ambitious country director in MI6. Then, quite suddenly, the figure of Herbert Perkins came into my mind. What would Bert be doing now, I wondered?

In fact, Herbert Perkins, or 'Bert' to friends, was doing exactly what he did every weekday morning. As regular as clockwork, he got up at six and made his wife Doris a cup of tea, which he left by her bed. He had his own breakfast of tea, toast and marmalade alone. Then he had a bath, shaved, and dressed carefully in a clean white shirt – Doris always left one out for him – his grey suit and his old army tie. He listened to the seven o'clock news on the BBC, went up to give Doris a goodbye kiss, and left the house at exactly a quarter past seven. He carried his old black briefcase in one hand, and a newspaper in the other. He walked to South Woodford underground station, and by half past seven he was sitting in a corner seat on the Central Line train, reading the sports pages. Anyone looking at him would think he was just another office worker, starting another day in a dull office job.

From the outside, he was indeed a grey man – in his mid-fifties, average height, glasses, his grey hair carefully combed to cover a bald patch – a typical example of middle-aged respectability. He had lived in the same house in Woodford for over 25 years – ever since he joined MI6 from the Army. His daily routine never changed – he left the house at a quarter past seven in the morning and returned at half past six in the evening. At weekends he would work in the garden, watch TV with Doris, and occasionally go down to the local pub for a beer.

Herbert Perkins was not, however, quite what he seemed to be. His father had been a sergeant-major in the Army. He had been a big man, with a big voice. When Bert finished secondary school, he wanted to go to university. His father would not hear of it.

'The Army was good enough for me, Bert. And it'll be good enough for you. Forget all these silly ideas about university. I'll get you into the Army – it'll make a man of you!'

Bert's mum made a weak attempt to change her husband's mind, but it was too late. At the age of 19, Bert went into the Army.

Bert was good at physics and maths so he went into the Signals Regiment – a unit dealing with all forms of communication in the Army. He was good, and soon afterwards he was moved to a special unit working on code-breaking. It seemed he had a special gift for this kind of work. Not long after that, MI6 discovered him. He transferred out of the Army, and into MI6. And so, at 25, Bert found himself decoding messages from Soviet nuclear submarines and East German agents.

One evening, he met Doris at a church dance. It was love at first sight. They married a year later, and a year after that, their son Peter was born. They moved into the house in Woodford, and life settled into a steady routine.

Bert's career steadily developed. He could never hope for

the very top jobs – he had no university degree. But those who do get the top jobs depend on people lower down in the organisation. They depend on people who can provide information at a moment's notice, who can recall events from far back in the past. People who act as the heart of the organisation's memory. Bert had become one of these key people. He was a sort of office manager – in charge of the details of operations, reporting, briefing and debriefing, and of the records. He was a grey spider sitting in the middle of a very large and sensitive web of information. There was not much he did not know about all the operations run by MI6 in the past 15 years or more.

He now worked in the large headquarters of MI6 next to the River Thames. And as usual, at exactly half past eight, Bert was arriving there.

Chapter 9 *Nina Rowlandson*

Nina Rowlandson was awake, lying in bed in the only hotel in Latouyrie. She had not slept well. The whole operation with Heid had turned into a nightmare. She had waited in that horrible, dirty little café until it had got dark. When she went outside to get some air, there was still no sign of Heid. What was worse, the car had gone. What had happened? She was stuck in the middle of nowhere with no transport, no luggage – it was all in the car Heid had hired – and no idea of what had happened to Heid. She suddenly felt cold and scared. She knew Dan well from the San Cristobal operation. They had even been lovers for a brief while during their escape. He had saved her life several times during that terrible journey through the jungle. She knew just how dangerous he could be.

She couldn't risk asking questions about Dan in the bar. She felt helpless. All she wanted to do was to get out of this place. Eventually she phoned for a taxi from Latouyrie, ten kilometres away. The village had a single hotel with a bad-tempered owner, uncomfortable beds, the smell of old cigarette smoke left by previous guests and noisy water pipes. By the time she arrived, it was too late for dinner. Instead, she went out for a walk. It was not a long walk as there were only two main streets, which crossed each other at a bridge, where two rivers joined. However, she did find what she was looking for – a public pay phone.

She pushed her phone card into the machine and dialled

the emergency number in London. She spoke quickly and urgently.

'Fox here.'

The voice on the other end was sharp and bad-tempered.

'Why are you calling, Fox? Is the hunt over?'

'No. I mean, I don't know. Our "friend" is missing and so is the car. I'm alone and I'm stuck in the middle of nowhere. I'll try to get to Paris by tomorrow. I feel we are in trouble. Big trouble.'

'Come back to London immediately. Use the "safe" house. Wait there till we send someone. Don't call again!' The line went dead.

She went back to her uncomfortable room. She could not stop thinking about what had happened. Her head was full of questions. Why had Strang forced her to go with Heid to kill Dan? Strang had told both of them that Dan was a threat to them. He said that Dan was about to release the story of the operation to the press. If he did that, their pictures would be all over the newspapers. If they did not kill Dan, they would lose their safe lives. But Nina wondered why Strang had not sent someone else. Perhaps he had some other reason. She did not trust him.

Nina spent the rest of the night trying to get to sleep. Every time she began to fall asleep, terrifying pictures would flash through her mind: Dan, still alive, gun in hand, chasing her through the streets. Then she was drowning in mud in San Cristobal – a boot pushing her head under the surface. The pictures played endlessly in the theatre of her mind. She could hear the cold voice of Cas, 'You stupid idiot! You didn't think I loved you, did you?' And Hugo Strang's upper class accent, 'You have no real choice, my dear. It's him, or you. If you don't do it, you'll lose everything. You decide.'

She tossed and turned, fighting her nightmares until, thankfully, daylight came through the thin curtains. There was a station in the town, though only two trains a day stopped there. Luckily there was a local train at eight, with a connection with the Toulouse to Paris express. She waited on the empty platform. She was the only passenger to board the train.

From then on, the return journey went smoothly: from Paris she took the Eurostar express train to London via the Channel Tunnel. But it was late evening before she let herself into the big Victorian house in Wimbledon, using the key Strang had given her. This was the 'safe' house, but somehow she did not feel safe there.

She took a long, hot bath, and fell into bed. Within minutes she was sleeping deeply.

Chapter 10 *Hugo Strang*

As Dan arrived at Gatwick airport, Hugo Strang was leaving his fashionable West London flat. He was a little late that morning, as he had entertained a group of visiting American politicians the night before. It had been a late night.

Strang was 45, slim, and classically handsome. Keeping fit was almost a religion with him. It was part of his competitive character. He was always perfectly dressed with a quiet but fashionable elegance. And always knowledgeable and charming – something that meant he had hundreds of friends. Needless to say, these friends were all high-flyers – leaders, just like him. And he treated ordinary people like rubbish, kicking them out of his way when necessary.

His friends greatly admired how much he knew, how well he spoke foreign languages. They also admired his clever jokes and his expensive lifestyle. But people who worked with him (or worse, worked for him) hated him for his ambition, his total selfishness and his pride.

Of course, he had all the right connections. His family had been rich landowners for centuries. He was educated at public school and Oxford University, leaving with a first class degree. He had been interviewed and chosen for MI6 as soon as he left Oxford. His sharp, cold mind and his skill at making himself useful to his superiors had led to immediate success. After working in Berlin, he had been moved back to London. There he became one of the inner circle of people who really made the important decisions. It was while he was head of the Latin American department in London that he had planned the San Cristobal operation.

Yet, although he was so successful, no one really trusted him. Perhaps that was why he was still not married. And many people asked themselves where he got all the money he needed to support his expensive lifestyle. There had also been that unfortunate event involving Peter Perkins, which had almost ruined him – but that was all a long time ago now. But people still talked about him – behind his back, of course.

As he entered his office, the phone rang.

'Strang?'

He recognised Sir Clive's voice immediately. It sounded angry and aggressive.

'What's going on? The woman called the emergency number last night. The operation in France went wrong. You promised me that everything would be taken care of. Our "friend" escaped. We don't know where he is. What are you going to do about it?'

'But, but, Sir, everything was planned down to the last detail. I don't see how it could possibly . . . '

'Well, it did go wrong. Very badly wrong. So how are you going to put it right? Daniel Combes is a double danger to us now. He knows what he knew before. That was why we needed to remove him. But now he also knows that someone tried to kill him – and it won't take him long to work out who was behind it all. So, you don't have long to take care of it. I can't afford to have all this in the newspapers. That's why we decided to deal with him in the first place.'

'I . . . er . . . I'll take care of it Sir. Don't worry. I understand.'

'I hope you do. If I go down, I'll take you with me. And by the way, I think you'll need to get rid of the woman, too. I've decided to get "you know who" back from the US. He can deal with her. We've already been in touch with him. He arrives this evening on the ten o'clock flight from New York. You'd better meet him. Make sure he knows what he has to do. And don't lose sight of him. We will need to deal with him too – later.'

Chapter 11   *Death in Berlin*

I had no problems coming through passport control at Gatwick. I couldn't make up my mind where to go first. In the end, I decided to head for somewhere near South Woodford. The memory of Bert Perkins had given me an idea. I hired a small car and set off eastwards on the boring M25 motorway which runs around London in a big circle. As I drove through the heavy traffic, I tried to think about what I should do next.

I suppose I could have just called Sir George, my former boss, and told him what had happened at the river in France. But that didn't seem like a very sensible thing to do. If Sir George already knew about the plan to kill me, I would be in greater danger. If Sir George didn't know about it, I would be drawing unnecessary attention to myself. Sir George? Maybe later, but not now.

I even thought about breaking into Hugo Strang's flat and beating the truth out of him. I was sure that Strang was involved somehow, though I could not work out how or why. But if I broke in and beat up Strang, they would know I was back in England. Anyway, what good would it do? I decided to deal with Strang later, too.

The only person I could really trust was Bert Perkins. We had always got along well in the old days, Bert and me. I always thanked him for what he did for us all. Other people often treated Bert like a servant, but not me. And we had become real friends during that terrible business with his son, Peter.

Peter was his only child, and Bert had given Peter the university education which his own father had prevented him from having. Peter was a brilliant student and graduated from University with a first-class degree in International Relations. In his final year, he had been approached by someone from 'a government organisation working for the good of the country.' They always did it like that. I always thought that employing Peter was a bit peculiar, though. MI6 didn't normally employ members of the same family. But of course, Peter had no idea what his father's real job was. Bert never spoke about his work at home. Someone, somewhere, must have known who Peter was, and who his father was, too. Yet Peter had been approached and he accepted the job.

His first job was in Berlin, where Hugo Strang was the MI6 Bureau Chief. It was just before the Berlin Wall came down. The political situation was dangerous. But life in West Berlin was exciting, and Peter soon settled down. He was a hard worker and often stayed late in the office. He got on well with Strang, although they were so different. Strang spoke highly of Peter and began to give him more and more responsibility. Some of the other people in the office were even a bit jealous of him, I found out later.

But then, something went wrong between them. No one was quite sure what it was, but Strang suddenly began to treat Peter badly. He gave him only the most boring jobs. And he openly criticised Peter's work in front of the others.

It was soon after this that Strang gave Peter a particularly difficult and dangerous operation. There is no doubt that he acted wrongly. Peter had never worked on this kind of operation, and Strang could easily have found a more experienced agent to do the job. At the inquiry into Peter's death, Strang argued that Peter had needed the field experience. Strang was never punished but the suspicion remained that something dishonest had gone on. Something which was never mentioned. Something which Strang wanted to cover up. Something which the inquiry wanted to cover up, too.

Peter's job was to arrange for the escape of a senior East German government official. The man had been passing valuable information to the Berlin bureau of MI6. He now suspected that he had been found out. He needed to get out as fast as possible. Peter had to help him escape.

Peter made arrangements for false papers and a car. But their car was stopped well before the checkpoint between East and West Germany. They shot the official as he tried to escape. Then they took Peter away for questioning. Soon after that the East Germans contacted the MI6 office. They said that they were interested in exchanging Peter for one of their own agents who was in prison in Britain for spying. This man's name was Holzmann, Gunther Holzmann. They badly wanted this agent back. He was obviously very important to them. London agreed and I was the one who was sent over to Berlin to arrange the prisoners' exchange.

I went to see Bert in his office before leaving for Berlin. Bert had no formal or official part in the exchange, but he knew about it. He was terribly upset. He needed support and he needed it badly. I spent several hours with him, listening to his worries, trying to set his mind at rest. I promised Bert I would do everything I could to bring Peter back safely.

But when I arrived in Berlin, there was a surprise waiting for me. My East German contact called me to say that the exchange was off. I spent over a week trying to find out why the East Germans had changed their minds, and trying to find out what had happened to Peter.

I got the answers to my questions in a dark and dirty bar in Tegel, a suburb of Berlin. I had arranged to meet Kurt Klassens there. Kurt was my oldest Berlin contact. He looked like a retired boxer, with scars on his cheeks and a broken nose. He wore a leather overcoat, smoked cigars, and drank beer followed by small glasses of strong apple schnapps. He was now on his fourth drink. Kurt was tough. I was never quite sure whose side he was on. When we needed information, he sometimes found it for us – if we paid him enough. Though I'm pretty sure he also provided the East Germans with information about us too – if they paid him enough. Yet I trusted him. He had never betrayed me – as far as I knew! And he knew his way around the dark, complicated world of Berlin spyland.

'I'm sorry, Dan, but the boy is dead. They said he was killed while trying to escape. But you know what that means.'

'But why did they call off the exchange?'

'That's the interesting bit. The way I heard it, it was your people who called off the exchange of Peter for their man Holzmann. A message came from your Berlin office – "no exchange". There was no explanation but I guess someone in London thought Peter wasn't valuable enough to exchange for Holzmann. Sorry, man. This Peter wasn't a friend of yours, I hope?'

'Not exactly, but I know his father. What's Holzmann like? Have you ever met him?'

'Once or twice. You know how it is, Dan. I do a bit of business over here, a bit over there too sometimes, if there's any money in it. I have to make a living somehow.'

'So what's he like? Why is he so important? Why would we want to keep him in Britain?'

'Well, he was one of their top spies – a sort of "master spy". But there might be other reasons, I suppose. They say he's number one in the drugs business too. You know, all the opium that comes from Afghanistan. It's like the old Silk Road from China. Only now it's not silk. It's heroin. Berlin is the crossroads between east and west. And Holzmann has all the right contacts in the east. He knows everyone. I can't confirm any of this, of course. It's just a theory. But maybe it has something to do with the case. I don't know. Maybe he has contacts in the west too. Who knows? Let's have another drink.'

He ordered more drinks.

'Here's to the end of the Wall!' he said, raising his glass. 'And the success of the free market! You can be sure that Holzmann will always be here with us and doing well, whatever the political situation is!' He laughed, drained his beer, threw his cigar into the ashtray, and left quickly by the back door.

When I got back to the Berlin office I tried everything to find out who the 'no exchange' message had come from. I questioned everyone but I didn't find anything. I even interviewed Strang. Of course, he said he knew nothing about it.

'How can you possibly think that anyone here would

even dream of doing such a disgusting thing?' he spat, when I asked him.

The evening before I was leaving for London, I realised I had left some papers at the office. I went back to get them. It was late, almost midnight. The security guard let me in. I heard voices coming from Strang's office. They were arguing. I picked up my papers and walked back to the lift. Strang's door was half open as I passed but the office lights were off. I looked in. The light from the street caught the face of Strang's visitor. It was somehow familiar. I had seen it before somewhere. But where? The two men were still deep in conversation, so I didn't think they saw me. I hurried downstairs and left the building. But the picture of the man's face lit by the street light stayed in my memory.

The day after I got back to London, I went to see Bert, this time at his home in South Woodford. Someone had already told him the bad news. He sat in an armchair with a dead, empty expression on his face. I tried to explain what I had done to get Peter back. Bert remained silent, his cup of tea cold on the table beside his chair. It was only as I got up to leave that he spoke, 'You're a good man, Dan. I know you did everything you could to find Peter. But someone is responsible for this. I'll find out who it is, even if it takes me years. And when I do find out, I'll know what to do about it. Thank you for everything, Dan.'

From that time on, Bert started to look like an old man. He still did his work in his usual professional way, but he seemed to have lost interest in life. The light in Bert and Doris' lives went out when Peter disappeared.

Chapter 12 *The San Cristobal Operation*

My thoughts were interrupted when a car braked suddenly in front of me. I realised I had been day-dreaming. I was already approaching the Dartford Tunnel, which runs under the River Thames, and the traffic was very heavy. As I moved slowly, I began to think about how we had all got involved in that San Cristobal business. Heid, Nina and me had all been part of the same team, so there had to be some connection between San Cristobal and the attempt to murder me – but what was it?

The four of us had been given our instructions by Hugo Strang in the main meeting room in MI6 headquarters, overlooking the Thames. He introduced us in turn: Nina Rowlandson, Jurgen Heid, Daniel Combes and Charles Cousins.

'You've never worked together before. And it's not likely you'll ever see each other again once this operation is over. I therefore suggest you tell each other as little as possible about yourselves. You have, of course, been specially chosen for this operation: Nina for her training in medicine, and . . .' he paused, with a faint smile on his lips, 'for her physical attractions. Heid for his telecommunications skills, Dan for his weapons and explosives knowledge, and last, but by no means least, Charles, or Cas, for his organisational qualities and his language skills. Cas will be your team leader.'

Cas smiled at us all as Strang named him as our leader.

He and Strang also exchanged looks. They seemed to be sharing some kind of joke. They obviously knew each other quite well already.

I remember looking carefully at each of my team mates. Nina was extremely beautiful – tall and slim, with olive-coloured skin, green eyes and long red hair. When she moved, it was like watching a cat move – smoothly and effortlessly. I could hardly take my eyes off her, though she carefully avoided eye-contact with me.

Heid was about my own height and build, with slightly square, Germanic features, and very blue eyes. His eyes were strange. They seemed to be looking in rather than looking out. He rarely spoke. In the months to come, I realised that he was an entirely private person – someone who never showed his true feelings, who never shared his thoughts, who never opened up.

Cas' personality was the complete opposite of Heid's. He was 'tall, dark and handsome', the sort of man women fall in love with easily. His eyes were dark and full of humour. His energy was like electricity running through his body. I noticed the way Nina kept looking at him – and I felt a little jealous.

Strang was clearly enjoying himself. He described his special operation like a schoolboy showing off a new toy.

'As you know, we work closely with the CIA in certain geographical areas, particularly in Asia. We also work together in operational areas such as drugs, weapons, terrorist groups, and that sort of thing.

The operation you will be working on is slightly unusual. Normally, the CIA deals directly with problems in Latin America. This time, however, they have asked us to act for them. There is no need for you to know the reasons for this. Just believe me that they are good reasons.

The Republic of San Cristobal was created in the wave of revolutions that flowed through Latin America in the late nineteenth century. It's small: less than two million people, most of them Indians. Physically it's less than half the size of Honduras. There's a flat coastal area, most of it covered by jungle, and banana plantations, and a central range of thickly forested mountains. Apart from bananas, about the only thing the country produces is coca. As you know, coca is the plant used to make cocaine. And the majority of this is smuggled into the USA.

San Cristobal is described as a democracy but in fact it's a military dictatorship. The President is Julio Ramon Menendez–Arroyo de Ybarra y Figueras. Most people just call him *El Jefe* – the Chief.

Now El Jefe won an election twenty years ago in highly suspicious circumstances, and he has been in power ever since then. Occasionally he holds another election – but votes are cheap and there is no organised political opposition. So, the President and his friends treat the place like their own property – they give the orders and collect the cash, and the Indians do the work, pay the taxes and keep quiet. People can simply "disappear" overnight in San Cristobal.

Well, this was the situation until about ten years ago. That was when one or two of the Indians, who'd been overseas to study, came back with some different ideas! One of them was called Raoul Guayateca. He formed a new party – the *Frente por la Libertad de Ixtulpaca* or FLI for short. He was a bit like the President in the sense that he wasn't interested in elections either. He wanted a revolution – so that he could establish a communist government in San Cristobal. He planned to give the country a new name, an Indian name, *Ixtulpaca*. The Indians would take over from the Spanish-speaking upper class. A better country and society would be created.

We've heard it all before, of course. It's the same old story. But that's when the Americans began to take a closer interest in San Cristobal. Before that, it was just a name on a map. But it was in an important geographical location. The Americans did not want it to fall into the wrong hands – and there were plenty of wrong hands in Cuba, just across the water from San Cristobal.

So, they invited El Jefe up to Washington, and signed an agreement for military cooperation with San Cristobal. This included the usual financial aid, in dollars. Naturally, El Jefe and his people were very happy to accept all this free money. The CIA, of course, knew that he was involved in cocaine smuggling, but they chose to do nothing about it – at least for a time. They supplied him with weapons and training for his army. In return, he had to keep the FLI revolutionary party under control.

This arrangement worked very well . . . until last year. Then after the elections in the US, things started to change. The new US President wanted to help democracy worldwide. He also needed to make some progress in the fight against drugs. At the same time, the FLI began to have some success in San Cristobal. And El Jefe started to lose control. The Americans began to worry. As El Jefe lost control of his country, the drugs business began to get out of control, too. At one point, the president of San

Cristobal was openly using military planes to drop drugs north of the border. He had to go. He was an embarrassment. But how could they get rid of him? And who would replace him?

And that's where we come in. Our job – or should I say, your job – is to go in and get rid of El Jefe. We'll do this by supporting the FLI and training the revolutionary group to bring down El Jefe. At the same time, you'll find out as much as you can about the FLI and their plans. Once El Jefe is dead, you get out quickly. You pass on all your inside knowledge about the FLI to the CIA – and they'll take care of the rest. The Americans will make sure the FLI does not last long.

Now there are a lot of details to go through but that's the main idea. We'll leave you on a nice quiet beach in San Cristobal at night. You'll be met by someone from the FLI.

Take this training of the FLI seriously. You've got make them believe that you're working with them.

Please remember that once you're in, you are on your own. We cannot help you if you get into trouble. The British government cannot afford to be publicly involved, and neither can the CIA. So make sure it goes well!

Now – any questions?' He did not wait long enough for a reply. 'Good! Then I'll hand you over to the support team for the operational details. I shall see you again on your return. Good luck.'

Chapter 13 *Epping Forest*

I left the M25 at the M11 junction and turned south towards London. There was a signpost to Epping and Woodford. I turned off there. I had to find a way of meeting Bert Perkins without being noticed. It was too risky to phone him. I decided to find somewhere quiet to stay, and to meet him off the train when he came back from London.

Just outside Epping I found a quiet motel. What I like about these places is that they are cheap, clean – and above all, impersonal. You check in, you pay in advance, you get your key, and they leave you alone. No one wants to know who you are or what your business is. Most of the customers are tired businessmen who check in late, go straight to bed, and leave early next morning.

As I unpacked my bags, I suddenly felt cold fear. Where was the brown envelope with the CDs? I looked everywhere for it but it was gone. For a moment my mind went blank – where were they? Then I realised what had happened. The envelope was still in the house at Sauvelagarde! In the darkness, I had left it by accident in the drawer of my kitchen table! The CDs were my insurance. They contained details of the San Cristobal operation, and a lot about Berlin and other information. I had kept them in case MI6 ever broke its promises to me. I had planned to release the information to the newspapers if that happened. Now they were hundreds of kilometres away in France. I knew that, somehow, I had to get the CDs back.

I had a shower and a rest, trying to forget about the CDs. I thought about my meeting with Bert. What would he say? What did he know? Would he agree to help me? I lay on the bed and fell asleep with these questions on my mind. When I woke it was already four o'clock. I knew Bert would not arrive at South Woodford station until about six o'clock. I decided to go for a walk in the forest.

There was that lovely autumn smell as I entered the forest – wood smoke and wet leaves. It reminded me of my childhood: the happy times before my parents were killed. Before I married Francoise. Before I joined this dirty profession. I thought about the wasted years – how I had ruined my life, how the years had flown by, how I had failed as a father to Annie. So much wasted time. So much I was sorry for. So much bitterness.

By six, I was sitting in the car near the station entrance. A train came in from the direction of London. The crowd of tired men with briefcases, and young women in business suits and high-heeled shoes poured out, their mobile phones pressed to their ears. Bert was not among them. Ten minutes later another train pulled in. Bert was one of the last people to walk out through the entrance. He began walking towards home, a grey figure, walking slowly with his head down, his eyes on the path in front of him.

I drove the car slowly alongside him, stopped and opened the passenger door.

'Bert, it's me. Get in.'

He had been deep in thought. He looked up, surprised.

'Dan? It's you? How strange. I was just thinking about you.' He got in.

'I need your help, Bert. Can we meet to talk?'

'Of course,' he said quietly. 'I don't think you'd better come home with me now, though. It wouldn't be safe. Drop me off at that corner over there, and we'll meet later, at a pub.'

Bert paused for a second. 'The King's Head,' he said, 'is a pub just on the other side of Epping. I don't usually go there and it's quiet. Eight o'clock?'

I nodded and Bert got out of the car and walked slowly away.

On my way back to the motel I stopped off at an Internet café to check my email. There was nothing. I mailed Annie.

Dear Annie,

Good to see you. Hope you got back OK.
I've mislaid forgotten something and may have to ask you to go and get it. Are you busy? Would you have time?

Take care,
Dad

I waited for half an hour but there was no reply.

Chapter 14   *Waiting in Wimbledon*

Nina got up late. She felt more tired than when she had gone to bed. The bad dreams had returned to disturb her sleep during the night. She showered and made coffee. There were some croissants in the freezer, and marmalade in the cupboard. She put two croissants in the microwave and had breakfast. There was plenty in the freezer for lunch, even wine in a rack in the corner. But what she really needed was clean clothes; her case was still in the car Heid had hired. But she couldn't go out. They had told her to wait until someone came.

She waited all morning but there was no sign of anyone. She thought about calling the emergency number again but decided against it. At two o'clock, she decided to make a quick trip into Wimbledon to buy some clean clothes. By four o'clock she was back in the dark, Victorian house, preparing supper. She poured herself a glass of champagne, and waited. The clock on the wall ticked loudly and it was starting to annoy her. Why hadn't anyone come yet?

The hours passed. She watched some television, made herself a sandwich, and even tried to read one of the novels in the bookcase. When the clock struck midnight there was still no one. By then she had finished the bottle of champagne and started a second bottle. Suddenly she felt exhausted. She slowly climbed the stairs to the bedroom and fell into a deep sleep.

*   *   *

Nina woke slowly. It was dark but she knew that someone was there in the room with her. She reached under her pillow for the pistol she had put there. A dark shape suddenly appeared by the bed. Before she could use the pistol, strong hands grabbed her wrists and held her tight. She struggled, her legs kicking against the bed, but it was no use. He was too strong for her.

'Nina. It's me. Don't you recognise me in the dark?'

The man switched on the bedside lamp, and let her go. As she turned to face him, her eyes grew wider.

'Cas? I can't believe this is happening. But . . . you're dead! I saw them shoot you in Bambacocha.'

She paused, waiting for Cas to explain, but his lips closed her mouth. She pressed herself against him.

'Oh Cas! Is it you? Am I dreaming? I thought I would never . . . Oh yes! I want you. Yes. I've waited so long for this.'

After love, they were quiet for a while. He held her close and she lay sleepily in his arms. Then, he gently led her from the bedroom and downstairs to the kitchen. As she sat in her bathrobe, he opened another bottle of champagne and took some bread and cheese from the fridge.

'Let's have a midnight feast,' he said, 'just like the old days.' The clock on the wall showed three o'clock. It was still like a dream for her. He had come back, at last, back from the dead.

'I don't know what to say, Cas,' she began. 'I thought you were dead – I saw you being shot. They told me someone would come here, but . . . you? I can't believe this is happening . . . How did you escape? And why didn't you ever contact me? It's been five years, Cas. Five long years since I last saw you.'

Cas said nothing. He simply smiled at her in that dreamy way she loved so much.

Eventually he spoke. 'I had to disappear, my darling. Believe me, it was too dangerous for us to be in contact.'

Nina now felt more confused than ever. She wanted to believe him. One part of her desperately wanted to believe him. But she wasn't a fool.

'Cas, I don't know what's going on. Help me. What has changed? If it was too dangerous for us to meet before, what has changed now? All those threats from Strang – and the orders to kill Dan. What is it all about?'

At the mention of Dan's name, Cas' expression hardened.

'I can't explain now. It's too soon. You'll understand everything later, my dear Nina. All I can say is that Dan knows something that puts us all in danger. Dan has to go. And the sooner, the better.'

'So, what do we do now, Cas? He must have got away from Heid. Where is Heid anyway?'

'Yes. He got away from Heid . . . and he got away from you.' His voice took on a cold edge, 'And where is Dan now? You don't seem to have been very successful, do you? Now it looks as if I'll have to do the job myself.'

'You don't understand, Cas. Heid was so sure he had hit Dan. He went to look for the body in the river. I waited for him but he didn't come back. Then I found that the car was gone. I panicked. I didn't know what to do. That's why I called London.'

'That was not what I expected from you. You are a trained agent and you behaved like a schoolgirl.' His voice rose dangerously, 'What's wrong with you?'

He didn't wait for Nina to answer. 'My guess is that Dan will show up again soon. He's too hot-headed to hide. He'll be angry and looking for whoever tried to kill him – and that means you, my dear. So, when he pops up, I'll be waiting for him. I have to go away this weekend – an important meeting. I'll leave early in the morning and come back on Monday morning. Then we'll decide what to do.'

He looked at her with his hard, cold eyes and she suddenly felt frightened. Then, his face changed again. He smiled his charming smile and said, 'So, my darling. Let's forget about it all until I get back, OK? Let's finish the champagne.' They drained their glasses. Then he took her in his arms and led her back upstairs. The clock showed half past four.

They made love again. She felt so relaxed that she immediately fell asleep in his arms. Soon she was sleeping deeply. She must have thought she was having another nightmare when he put the pillow on her face, and held it there until she stopped struggling.

Cas took a shower and dressed. Before leaving the bedroom, he checked one last time that she was dead. Then he went downstairs, let himself out of the house, and drove away into the darkness.

Chapter 15 *At the King's Head*

The King's Head pub was only a kilometre from my motel. It too was in the forest – a traditional country pub. It felt warm and welcoming as I stepped through the door. There were a couple of men at the bar drinking beer. Otherwise, no one. I saw Bert at a corner table. He had a glass of beer in front of him. A glass of wine stood opposite him.

'Pinot Grigio,' he said. 'I seem to remember you rather liked that.'

'Thanks Bert. It's good to see you. Thanks for coming.'

'My pleasure, Dan. I owe it to you. I can't stay too long – we might attract attention.' Bert paused and drank some of his beer. 'So what's going on, Dan?'

'Heid and Nina came after me in France. I had to kill Heid, but I've no idea where Nina is now. I don't know who sent them, but I'm sure Strang is involved somehow. And maybe someone higher up. Maybe someone in the government. I was hoping you might have some information.'

'Any ideas about why Strang, or whoever, wants to kill you so badly?'

'That's what I've been asking myself ever since Heid shot at me. I can't think of an answer.'

'Well,' Bert said, 'my guess is that you know something. But perhaps you don't consciously know that you know it. And what you know makes life dangerous for them.'

'You mean, I've seen something, or know something that

puts them all in danger? Something I may not know about? Perhaps it's a connection that I haven't made yet – between them and someone or something else?'

'If I were you, I'd think back very carefully. Anything to do with Strang? Maybe something to do with an earlier operation.'

The ghost of an idea flashed through my mind. Something to do with Berlin; two men arguing in a dark office. But it was gone before I could catch it.

'Perhaps it's something related to San Cristobal, Dan,' Bert offered.

'San Cristobal? You know something, Bert. Tell me.'

Bert's face suddenly became tense and serious. 'I'm in this too, you know, Dan. When Peter was murdered, I found out it was Strang who called off the exchange. I've been waiting, Dan, waiting for the right moment. But now I think the time has come to get even with Strang. I don't care what happens to me any more. I want Strang fixed – once and for all. So you do your bit, Dan, and I'll do mine.'

'Thanks, Bert. I'm listening.'

'Here's what I've found out,' Bert began. 'I knew there was something going on. As I told you, I keep a very close watch on what Strang does, and he's been acting strangely for the last few days – very nervous and worried. So I did some more checking. It took me a while to get into their computer files but when I did I found plenty of interest.

First – Cas is still alive! His "death" at Bambacocha was obviously just a trick to make everyone think he was dead. He's been living in the USA in a small town in Vermont.

Second – Strang is right in the middle of all this. He recently contacted Cas in America and Cas is flying back.

Lastly, Strang used the other two – Nina and Heid – to get rid of you. He told them that you were going to sell the story of the San Cristobal thing to a Sunday newspaper. Apparently you were going to make a lot of money. Strang contacted the other two and brought them to London – Nina was in Crete and Heid in Germany. They didn't have much choice. He must have threatened them. If they didn't agree to get rid of you, they would lose their income from MI6, their protection, everything!

But Strang's plan went wrong. Now you've told me I know what happened. I'm also sure there is someone higher up who's involved. He must be feeling even more frightened than Strang. And I don't think it's Sir George. Do you have any ideas?'

My mind was racing. Cas still alive? But I had seen him die in Bambacocha. Someone higher up? But who could that be? And why were they worried about me? What did I know that could possibly be a threat to them?

'Let's have one more, shall we? Then I must get away.' Bert went through to the bar with the empty glasses.

He returned a few minutes later with two more drinks.

'Thanks for all of this, Bert. I always felt Strang and Cas were up to something. But it's a shock to find that Cas is still alive. Where do I go from here?'

'Well, one other bit of information I picked up is that there's some sort of secret high-level meeting planned between our people and the Americans. It's this weekend. And it'll be at Burstead House in Oxfordshire. I think you know the place.'

'Of course I do, Bert. It's where they took us for the debriefing after San Cristobal. It looks just like a traditional old English country house. All very innocent-looking. It certainly doesn't have an advertisement on the gate saying "Top Secret MI6 Briefing Centre"! But the security is tight. There are electronic alarms and dogs everywhere.'

'That's right. They only use it for really secret stuff. Strang will be there. Among others. Maybe you should pay them a visit? A nice quiet weekend in Oxfordshire?'

'Thanks, Bert. Sounds good. I'll need a gun, though.'

'I thought you might need some equipment. When I go, I'll leave my briefcase on the floor. I think you'll find the contents will come in useful.'

'Bert, you think of everything. Thank you.'

'I must get home now. Doris will wonder where I am. Take care – these people are dangerous.'

He stood up to leave. 'Oh, and by the way, Nina is staying in the safe house in Wimbledon. Do you remember it? There's a key in my briefcase. My guess is she's waiting for further instructions. She must be feeling pretty scared. I would be! Maybe you'd better get to her before Cas does. She might just be scared enough to tell you something useful.'

Bert's voice softened. 'Goodnight Dan. Stay in touch.'

Bert made his way slowly through the empty bar and out into the autumn night. I finished my drink. The two men at the bar were still deep in conversation. I picked up the briefcase and left.

Chapter 16   *Death in Wimbledon*

When I got back to the motel, I suddenly felt exhausted. I thought about driving down to Wimbledon immediately, but quickly decided against the idea. I needed some rest first.

The next morning I left early. I decided it would be quicker to take the Central Line train into London and the District Line out to Wimbledon.

After over an hour spent with commuters making their way to work, I arrived at Wimbledon station. The house was within walking distance. I remembered it from before. It was in a quiet side street – a square, dark, depressing, Victorian house with a high brick wall which surrounded a large garden with tall, dark trees.

There was no sign of life from the house, so I walked quickly up the drive and went round to the back door, keeping out of sight among the trees.

I looked in through the kitchen windows. On the table I could see two wine glasses and an empty bottle of champagne. I decided to take a chance and rang the doorbell. I could hear it echoing through the house. No answer. I rang again. Still no one came. I returned to the back door and let myself in with the key. Slowly and carefully I made my way to the front of the house and up the stairs. The main bedroom door was wide open. My heart sank as I saw the body on the bed. I had come too late. Nina would not be able to answer my questions. I was angry with myself. If only I had come the night before, I might have been able to save her life.

I went over to the bed. She was naked, and even in death, beautiful. The blue colour in her skin showed how she had died. The killer had left nothing in the bedroom as a clue. Her clothes were left neatly on a chair. Everything looked normal – except the dead body. I covered Nina with the sheet and went back downstairs.

I looked around the kitchen. The two glasses on the table suggested that she had known her killer. It was then that I noticed the cigarette end in the ashtray. Nina did not smoke. And there was no mistaking the unusual Turkish brand of cigarettes that Cas had always smoked. So Cas was back! And he had not wasted any time! I felt a great wave of anger run through me. Cas would have to pay for this with his own life.

I left the house and was locking the back door when I heard the sound of a car pulling into the drive. I crouched down and slowly and carefully looked around the corner. It was a white unmarked van with no windows. Two men got out and one took a stretcher from the back of the van. They entered the house through the front door and two minutes later, they came out with Nina's body on the stretcher, covered with a blanket. As soon as the van had gone, I walked quickly away towards the station.

Before taking the train back, I again went to an Internet café to check my email. There was a message from Annie.

Dear Dad,

It was great to see you. I got back OK.
I'm afraid I can't do anything for you at the moment. Lucien

and I have split up. It happened when I got back. I told him I was pregnant. All he said was 'Get rid of it then'. He was horrible to me. I want this baby, Dad. I can't believe this is happening to me. I'm sorry to worry you with this but I don't know what to do. I wish I could talk to you. I feel very lost at the moment. Please get back to me when you can.

Love
Annie

I was knocked over by Annie's news. Why hadn't she told me about the baby when we were in Barcelona? I decided I had to buy a mobile phone. I had to be able to speak to Annie at any time. I found a shop and within half an hour I had a new phone – one that no one could know was mine. But when I called Annie's number, there was only a recorded message. Where was she?

Chapter 17 *Burstead Hall, Oxfordshire*

On Saturday morning, I was on the M40 and heading towards Oxford. I was glad I had hired a small car. It would be ideal for driving through the narrow, winding country roads of north Oxfordshire. And it would not attract attention.

Two hours later, I was deep in the countryside northwest of Oxford. I stopped for lunch at a pub in Burstead. I was wearing casual walking clothes, so it was easy to mix with the lunchtime crowd of local people, hikers and tourists. I didn't think it was very likely that anyone from the Hall would be at the pub at lunchtime; they would all be busy preparing for the meeting.

The village was like a picture postcard. It was the sort of place tourists imagine when they think of England. The cottages and houses faced the village green. Their gardens were full of late summer flowers, giving the place a perfume like honey. There was a small stream below the village. It ran on through thick woods.

Burstead Hall was about a kilometre farther up the valley. The same stream ran through the gardens surrounding the house. That gave me an idea. This would be my way in to Burstead Hall. After lunch, I parked the car outside the village and set off on foot through the woods towards the Hall. I recalled my commando training as I moved swiftly and silently to a point where I could look down on the Hall.

The house was familiar to me. We had all spent two

weeks there after getting out of San Cristobal. It was a seventeenth century house with an elegant central building and two equally elegant wings, forming a U shape. I remembered that the central building was one large, high hall, used for meetings and dinners. The wings contained offices and kitchens on the ground floor, and bedrooms on the first floor.

Looking down, I could just see half a dozen large black cars parked in front of the house. The guests had arrived. Now would be the time for a few short meetings. There would probably be some kind of formal dinner that evening. The main meeting would probably be on the Sunday.

I walked carefully around the fence surrounding the house. It was almost three metres high, and impossible to climb. If I cut the fence in any way, the alarm would go off. If that happened, the guards, and their dogs, would come running.

I continued around the fence until I found what I was looking for. At the place where the stream ran under the fence, there was a small space. It had been a hot, dry summer, and the stream was very low. There was hardly any water under the fence. I would be able to make the space big enough to creep under the fence and into the gardens, without setting off the alarm. It was dangerous but I didn't have any other choice.

I went back to the car. I checked on places I could park. I needed a place out of sight of the guards at the main gates. Then I drove into the nearby town to do some shopping. I bought some rope, some petrol, and some small hand towels. Then I collected some empty bottles from the bottle bank in the supermarket car park. I was almost ready.

By seven o'clock I was back at Burstead Hall. I left the car under the trees in the place I had identified earlier. I reversed the car into the space – I thought I might need to get away fast. It was only 200 metres to the gates but the car was hidden by a bend in the road. I took the petrol, the bottles and the towels with me to a place farther into the woods, where no one could see me from the road. Then I made ten petrol bombs, carefully filling each bottle with petrol and finishing by pushing pieces of towels into each one as a fuse. I hid them under some dry leaves.

I carefully climbed down the steep slope to the stream bed. Within a few minutes, I had removed enough sand and stones to widen the space under the fence. Flat on my stomach, I crept under the fence. So far, so good. It was beginning to get dark. The security lights would go on soon, so I ran quickly across the open area of grass and hid myself in some bushes near the back entrance to the south wing of the Hall. I was only just in time: the whole of the grounds were suddenly bathed in bright light. I knew that one of the guards would normally make an inspection of the grounds soon after the lights went on. I watched from my hiding place. Sure enough, a few minutes later, a tough-looking guard appeared at the fence. Luckily, he did not have a dog with him. He jumped over the stream bed without noticing my entry point, and continued out of sight up the slope behind the Hall.

Dinner would be at eight o'clock in the main hall. I timed my move for a quarter past eight. By then there would be no one in the south wing. I settled down in the bushes to wait.

Chapter 18   *Big Fish: Deep Waters*

The lights had gone on in the main hall, and I could see figures moving about inside. I used the side door which led into a long corridor. At one end, there was a door into the hall itself. Next to it, some small stairs led to a balcony. I ran quickly and silently up the stairs, and crouched down in the semi-darkness. Below me I could hear the guests talking over pre-dinner drinks. And I could just see the figures through the bars surrounding the balcony. What I saw made me draw a sharp breath of surprise.

There were only six of them. Strang was easily identifiable in his elegant evening dress. He was offering a glass of champagne to a bald, middle-aged man who I recognised as Henry Minelli, a top presidential adviser. This man was very close to the US President, and spoke to him daily. Next to him was the tall figure of Sir Clive Horley, Private Secretary to the Minister for Defence in the British government. Suddenly I recognised him as the man arguing with Strang in his darkened office in Berlin all those years ago. Why hadn't I made the connection before? In a corner, talking to another man who had his back turned to me, I could see Bob Nash, head of the CIA. But who was the other man? Cas was also there, standing on the edge of the group. That was surprising. What was he doing here among these big fish?

One person I might have expected to see was Sir George. However, he wasn't there. Maybe he was not part of this thing at all. That would make sense. In a way, I felt more confident when I realised this. He, at least, was 'clean'.

A waiter appeared at the other door and announced that dinner was served. The group moved towards the central table, set with elegant silverware and crystal glasses, and bowls of pink and yellow roses. It was then that I got my first sight of the man who had had his back turned. I could hardly believe my eyes. It was Holzmann! Holzmann the master spy. Holzmann, the man who had been offered in exchange for Peter.

Suddenly my memory began to stir again. I remembered my last conversation with Kurt Klassens in that dark bar in Tegel. Something he had said about Holzmann. Something to do with the Mafia? Drugs? The new 'silk road'? If it was drugs, then it might explain why the CIA was there. What was the connection between that and the attempt to kill me? San Cristobal, of course! Drugs from the east through Germany and the old Soviet empire. Drugs from the west through US support of dishonest and corrupt governments in Latin America. And where did the drugs go? Mainly to the USA – but to Europe, too. Heroin going from east to west. Cocaine going in the opposite direction. And top officials were fully involved in both businesses. People at the top who were making a lot of money behind their respectable positions. People like Sir Clive perhaps. And they would feel terribly threatened by anyone who might have made the connection. By anyone who might make their secrets public. I had been in Berlin at a time of opportunities – and Strang (and his boss, Sir Clive, probably) had been all too ready to take them. And I had been in San Cristobal too, seeing the other end of things. It was obvious to me now that San Cristobal had been a suicidal operation – we were supposed to die. None of us, except Cas, should have survived. We all knew too much. And now, these people obviously saw me as a threat.

My mind was now racing. I had to find Bert, get hold of Kurt Klassens again, check my suspicions. But first, I had to try to overhear as much of their conversation as possible. It wasn't easy. Several of them were talking at once. There was a noise of plates and knives and forks. All I could hear were bits and pieces of what they said, 'What are we going to do now then?', 'How come you didn't take care of this back in Bambacocha?', 'Where is he now?', 'What do you mean, you don't know? We have to know!', 'Maybe he hasn't made the connection. Maybe we're worrying about nothing.', 'What happened to the girl?', 'We can't afford any more mistakes, Strang. Your head is on the block – and so is mine if this gets out . . .'

A strong voice came through the noise.

'Let's calm down, gentlemen. We have until tomorrow morning to work out a plan of action. Don't let's spoil a good dinner.'

It was Sir Clive. The conversation turned to other matters, and I decided to leave quietly. I had work to do before Sunday morning.

Chapter 19   *Settling Accounts*

I checked in to a small hotel in North Oxford. I badly wanted to talk to Bert but I dared not risk a phone call. I would have to make do with email again. I went into town to find an Internet café.

Dear Bert,

I need some information. What do you have on Sir Clive Horley? And is Kurt Klassens still around? How do I contact him? Any information on drugs traffic in Berlin around the time of the Wall coming down?

More later,
Dan

While I was waiting, I tried to call Annie again. She was still not there. I was desperate to hear from her, so I sent her a long email instead. I tried to offer her some comfort, but it wasn't easy to do at a distance. I knew that she needed more than just words on a computer screen. She needed me. Maybe it was the first time since she was a child that she really needed me. I had let her down then. I could not let her down again. Somehow, I had to get to her. But first I had to deal with Cas and Strang.

I went out for a drink and a snack. Then I went back to the Internet place again. There was no message from Bert. I couldn't wait any longer so I returned to the hotel.

It was a sleepless night. Scenes from the past flashed through my mind. Voices echoed in my ear. My mind boiled and bubbled with fantasies and facts. I relived each of the events that might help me solve the puzzle: the visit to Berlin, my conversation with Klassens in that bar, the briefing with Strang, the San Cristobal operation, Cas' 'death', the murder attempt at the river in France, the dinner party at the Hall . . . Everything went round and round in my mind as I tossed and turned through the night. And mixed up with these scenes, pictures of Annie as a little girl, crying; Annie as a young woman reaching out to me from the whiteness of a hospital room . . .

I left early the next morning. It was eight o'clock when I reversed the car quietly into the place under the trees near the Hall. I packed the petrol bombs in a rucksack, checked the pistol Bert had found for me, and set off for the stream again. The place under the fence by the stream was still as I had left it. It had not been discovered. I crept under it quickly and crossed to my hiding place in the bushes. There was no one around.

I entered the Hall through the door to the south wing again, and went up to the first floor. There was no sign of life. This was where the guest bedrooms were but I had no idea who was in which room. Then I heard footsteps coming up the stairs. I hurriedly hid the rucksack behind some curtains at the top of the stairs and stood in the shadows. One of the servants came up the stairs carrying a tray with breakfast on it. He went along the corridor and knocked on a door. A voice called out.

'Coming. Just a minute!'

I recognised Cas' voice. The door opened, and the tray was taken. The servant made his way back down the corridor towards my hiding place.

I acted without thinking. When the man reached the top of the stairs, I tapped him lightly on the shoulder from behind. As he turned his head, I hit him hard on the side of the neck. He fell to the floor instantly. I pulled him behind the curtains and took off the jacket of his uniform. I put it on. Then I fitted the silencer on to my pistol and walked slowly along the corridor to the door of Cas' room.

I felt the anger in me rising like a dark tide. Cas had tried to have me killed. Strang and Cas were still planning to kill me. I thought of Peter and how his death had destroyed the lives of Bert and Doris. I thought of Cas' murder of Nina. She and I had only been lovers for a short time – and she and Heid had tried to kill me. But I still felt for her. She had suffered too. I was furious at the deliberate evil of these two men. My mind was full of one thing only: revenge. I wanted them to pay for what they had done – to me, to Peter, to Bert, to Nina . . .

I knocked on the door.

'Who is it?' This time it was Strang's voice.

'Room service. We forgot your newspaper,' I said.

'You get it,' said Strang's voice.

Cas opened the door. He was wearing just a towel and his hair was still wet from the shower.

'Surprised?' I said. I didn't give him a chance to reply. I shot him in the stomach. His face was frozen in shock. This was not part of his plan. He fell back into the room, holding his stomach, blood already visible through his fingers. Strang was sitting at the table, eating his breakfast. When he heard the 'phut' of the bullet and saw Cas falling backwards, he jumped up, upsetting his breakfast tray all over the floor. I shot him in the stomach, too. He fell back on the bed, his blood bright red against the white of the bed sheets.

Neither man made any attempt to call out. They lay crying with pain.

'I've been waiting a long while for this,' I said. 'Your games are over.'

Cas made a weak attempt to get up and I shot him again. In the chest. Then once more, in the head. He did not move again.

Strang began to shake with the shock. 'Don't kill me. Don't kill me! I can explain everything. It isn't what you think. I was trying to save you. You know how cruel Cas is . . . I tried my best to stop him but . . .'

There was another 'phut' sound as I shot him. This time in the shoulder.

'Don't bother lying to me!' I said. But as I raised the gun to fire one last shot the telephone rang. At the same time I heard a voice from the next room.

'You OK in there?'

'Fine,' I called. But I lost my concentration for a moment and Strang managed to move behind the bed. My shot hit him in the knee. Strang would not walk without pain again. But he was not dead.

The phone stopped ringing. There was a noise from the next room again. It was time to go. As I reached the landing, another door opened and I heard someone call out, 'Hey there. What's going on? You guys OK?'

I didn't wait to reply. I grabbed the rucksack, took out one of the petrol bombs, lit it with my lighter, and threw it down the corridor towards the voice. There was a blinding flash, then flames quickly spread along the corridor.

I ran quickly down the stairs and opened the door into the main Hall. It was set out for the meeting. I threw another petrol bomb into the room. Flames licked up the long curtains and the wooden walls. There was confused shouting as guests tried to leave their rooms. There was smoke everywhere. People ran about, bumping into each other, looking for fire extinguishers. In the confusion, no one noticed me in my servant's uniform jacket. I threw the last petrol bomb into an office on the ground floor. Instantly it burst into flames.

I opened the back door and looked around. There were no guards in sight. Probably they were all at the front of the Hall. Flames were now licking all along the back of the building and black smoke was coming from the first floor windows.

I ran quickly across the grass and back to the stream. Looking back, I could see the guards running towards the Hall. When I reached the place where I had parked the car, I stopped suddenly. There was another car parked right next to it – an old Ford. I dropped to my knees and began to creep in a circle towards the car. As I reached the car, Bert stepped out from behind a tree.

'I think you need some help,' he said. 'Get in.'

We reached the top of the road just in time. Three fire engines came racing along from the direction of Oxford and turned into the narrow road, their lights flashing and alarm bells ringing. Just behind them came the blue flashing lights of two police cars.

Chapter 20 *Talking it over*

'I got your email,' said Bert. 'I thought perhaps I'd better come in person because I don't think we have much time left. It looks as if you needed some help anyway. Tell me what happened back there. Did someone drop a match? Or was someone smoking in bed?' He grinned.

I told him briefly what had happened.

'I lost control, Bert. I know I should have stayed cool but I'd bottled up all the tension and the anger – it got the better of me. I'm afraid I've made a mess of things.'

Bert nodded. 'It's a pity you didn't kill Strang, though. He could give us a lot of trouble. Once they get over the confusion of the fire, and when they find Strang – if they do – there's going to be big trouble. They'll be looking for you everywhere. In fact, I think we'd better get off the M40 right now, just in case.' He turned off and took minor roads towards London.

'Where are we heading, Bert?'

'Well, I think I'd better get you out of the country before they catch up with you. We're lucky it's Sunday, so a lot of people are off work, and the confusion back there will delay them for a few hours. But I'll feel happier if you're on the other side of the Channel before tomorrow. My brother-in-law, Jeff, has got a small sailing boat down at Whitstable on the coast. He often sails across to France. I'm going to ask him to take you over with him.' He pulled in at a petrol station, filled up with petrol and then went to a pay phone. Five minutes later he was back.

'Good. Jeff will take you to France. He's retired you know. So he's got lots of time on his hands. I've told him you're running away from your wife. He likes that idea. Jeff ran away from his own wife a long time ago! He's a bit odd but he'll get you there.'

'Thanks Bert.'

'By the way, you asked for information on Kurt Klassens. Funny you should mention him again. When I checked on him, I discovered that he was dead. He died just after your last meeting with him. The petrol tank of his car exploded on the way back into Berlin from Tegel. Nasty "accident", wasn't it? What do you make of that?'

'I guess it all adds up. That conversation was more important than I thought at the time. Someone must have known about my meeting with Klassens. They obviously thought that he told me something in that bar – something that he shouldn't have. Something dangerous for them. That's why they killed him. Now I think I know what it was. Something you said to me in the pub the other night stuck in my mind. You said I might know something I didn't know that I knew. Something crossed my mind about Berlin then. When I saw Holzmann, there in Burstead Hall, all the pieces of the jigsaw puzzle fell into place. Listen and tell me if it makes sense. When I spoke to Klassens, he mentioned Holzmann's connections with the Soviet Union. Now, Holzmann knew, just like we all knew, that the East German government was nearly finished. He wanted to get back to Berlin to take advantage of the situation, to make sure that the drugs business stayed in the right hands, to use his connections . . . all of that. But he couldn't do that because we were holding him. Now, supposing someone on our side wanted to use Holzmann and his connections to get a share of the drugs business? Something Klassens said made me think of this. He mentioned that Holzmann might have contacts in the West.'

'But he didn't say who they were, did he?' asked Bert.

'No, he didn't. Anyway, suppose Holzmann wouldn't agree? And suppose this someone, a senior someone in London, worked out a plan to force Holzmann to agree?'

'What do you mean?' asked Bert again.

'Well, first they pretend that they're going to exchange him. So they set Peter up, and he is offered in exchange for Holzmann. Holzmann is delighted that he'll soon be back home. But then, they suddenly cancel all the arrangements. Holzmann is told that the exchange is off – unless . . .'

'You mean unless he agrees to give the man in London a share?' said Bert.

'Right. After a week of this, he agrees to cooperate. A week after that, they free him and he flies back to East Berlin. By then it's too late for Peter – the East Germans have shot him. But "they" don't care. Peter wasn't important.'

'I can't believe it. I . . . can't believe it,' said Bert.

'I know. I'm sorry, Bert. It's hard to believe that one human being could just throw away another human life, just like that. Anyway, the next month, the Berlin Wall comes down, and our friends Strang and the shadowy someone, with Holzmann, are in business – very profitable business. The drugs business.'

'So it was all about money? And Peter had to die so that they could get their hands on more dirty money?'

'I know. It seems so. I'm so sorry, Bert. After this, I think our shadowy friend in London starts to get really greedy. He has connections with some of the Washington people who are involved with the Latin American drug scene, just as Strang is in with the former Soviet Mafia. Why not get together? One of the key links is San Cristobal. They need to get rid of El Jefe and replace him with someone who won't be an embarrassment, but who will continue to play the game. And so the four of us were all sent to San Cristobal.'

'And by then, Strang was in charge of the Latin American department, wasn't he? I wonder if the shadowy high-up arranged for him to get that job. It was very convenient for their plan,' said Bert.

'You're probably right. Of course, our friends didn't intend that we should ever come back. We were supposed to "disappear" – all of us except Cas, of course. Because Cas knew everything, and Strang couldn't do without him. But unfortunately for our friend Strang, we didn't die after all. We were a serious embarrassment. He couldn't get rid of us because Sir George knew we were back. And I don't think Sir George had anything to do with this. So, they sent us all away, instead. We didn't know enough to threaten our friend Strang – or so he thought – so we were safe enough as long as we played by the rules. What puzzles me is why they suddenly changed their minds. Why send Nina and Heid to kill me? I hadn't made a move in five years. I hadn't said or done anything to threaten them.'

Bert said nothing for a while. He was biting his lip, and his eyes were shining with tears.

'My son,' he said. 'My son died because of all this.' Bert

turned to Dan, 'You've done your bit. Tomorrow, I'll start to do mine. I'll tell everyone about the lot of them, including that Sir Clive Horley. I checked on him and I think I may have the answer to your question. A few weeks back, there was a very difficult question in Parliament during question time. A member of parliament wanted to know about stories that the government had been involved in sending special forces and weapons to support revolutionary groups in San Cristobal. He asked if these stories were true. If so, who was responsible? I don't know where he got his information, but it sent shock waves through the government. Later on a government spokesman denied any involvement. The name of the spokesman? Sir Clive Horley! They were lucky the press didn't follow it up. But this must have made our friends very nervous indeed.'

'I'll bet it did,' I said.

'I bet that's when they decided there were too many people alive who had information on the San Cristobal operation. And that's why they tried to have you killed. If Heid and Nina had managed to kill you, they would have no doubt had "accidents", too.'

Chapter 21   *Crossing the Channel*

Whitstable is a little town on the north Kent coast. It's still famous for its seafood, especially oysters. Not much happens in Whitstable. There are a few fishing boats still and lots of sailing boats. Most of the people who live there are retired.

Jeff, Bert's brother-in-law, was one of them. But he was far from ordinary. Unlike Bert, he was a big man, with long dark hair tied at the back. He also had a long beard, and a loud, cheerful voice. He lived in a little cottage near the harbour where he kept his boat.

'Come on in, Bert. Nice to see you. Hello there! You must be Bert's friend. Sorry to hear about your trouble with the wife. Who needs women anyway?' He delivered his last comment with a broad grin. 'Let's have a drink. I haven't seen you for ages, Bert. How's life?' He pulled open a large cupboard lined with rows of bottles of all shapes and sizes. 'What'll you have?'

*   *   *

Several hours later, Bert got up to leave.

'You've had too much to drink. You can't drive now,' said Jeff. 'You'd better stay the night. I can't leave until the early morning tide anyway. We'll get going at five thirty. With a bit of luck, we'll be over the other side by lunchtime. So let's all get a bit of sleep, shall we? Bert, you can have the spare room. Dan, you can sleep on the sofa. I'll give you a call when it's time to go. I must just go down to the harbour and make sure everything's OK for the trip. I'm going to enjoy this.'

While he was out, Bert made a call to Doris on Jeff's phone. He spoke little, but something she told him obviously worried him.

'She says there have been several phone calls asking for me. They wouldn't say who they were. I don't like the sound of it.'

'I hope all this won't get you into trouble, Bert.'

'Don't you worry about me,' he said in a determined voice. 'I know how to take care of myself. The main thing is you – just make sure you get clear. It will be better if we don't communicate again – at least for quite a long time. You must have plans about where you're going, but it's better you don't tell me. I'll do what I can over here. I'll be visiting some newspapers as soon as I can. They'll love this story. And that will be the end of Strang and Horley.'

'OK. I'll say goodbye now then, Bert. Thanks for everything, and take care.' We shook hands.

Before sleep, I tried once again to call Annie. Still there was only the recorded message. What was going on? I fell asleep worrying about her all alone with her problems . . . and about how I would get my CDs back.

It was still dark when we left in the morning. Bert had set off home even earlier. Jeff's old boat moved out of the harbour using the engine. When we were well clear of the coast we put up the sails and set off eastwards – for France.

'I'm going to head for Dunkirk,' said Jeff. 'It's not the nearest port, but it's the most convenient from here. And I have a young lady friend who lives there. So, if you don't mind . . .'

There was a good fresh wind and we were quickly sailing out of the Thames Estuary and into the Channel. Soon we were crossing some of the busiest shipping lanes in the world. Huge container ships and oil tankers passed, their engines loud above the sound of the sea. In the distance I could see the ferry boats leaving Dover on their way to Calais. It was like being on a great watery motorway.

It took us five hours to reach Dunkirk. Jeff knew his way around and steered his boat into a vacant place in the marina. The marina was half empty. Winter was approaching, and a lot of boats had already been pulled out of the water for repainting and repairs.

'You just stay here, out of sight for a bit, OK?' said Jeff. He went off towards the harbour buildings to pay the harbour fees. He came back twenty minutes later.

'I think maybe I'll say goodbye now,' he said with a grin. 'I've got some business to attend to, if you see what I mean! I mustn't keep the lady waiting.'

I thanked him, and quickly made my way out of the marina gates. I hurried into town and found a quiet restaurant where I could stay off the streets for a time.

Chapter 22 *Driving South*

After lunch I rented a car and drove off towards the south east. Bert had said that I must have plans but in fact, I had no real idea of what to do next. I knew that somehow I had to get the CDs back from Sauvelagarde. Once I had them, I would feel safer. If necessary I could use them as an insurance policy to threaten the people who were after me. They would do almost anything to stop Bert's accusations from being supported by evidence. But where would I go? Where would I hide? And now, there was the added complication of Annie. I knew that any plans I made must include her. I couldn't just leave her again. I needed somewhere quiet to work things out properly before I made my move to get back the CDs.

I thought about what to do as I drove across Flanders. Flanders is flat. Flanders is dull. The sky seems to weigh down on the earth like a big, grey blanket. Flanders is history. Millions of young men died here and there are many First World War graves all over the countryside. Flanders itself is also dying; its factories are closed down, its workers unemployed. It is a depressed and depressing region. As I drove across it, I became more and more worried about the future – my future and Annie's future.

But, as I got farther south, the countryside slowly started to develop into small hills and valleys. And there were no more dead industries, just farms and fields – green fields full of fat, happy-looking cows – and great forests. My mood began to improve.

When evening came, I stopped in a small town and took a room in a hotel overlooking a river. I suddenly felt tired. After dinner, I went straight to my room and fell into a deep sleep.

Late the next morning, I called Annie's number again. This time, she answered. It was a tired, lifeless voice.

'Hello Dad. Thanks for your emails.'

'Where have you been Annie? I was worried about you. I've been phoning you but all I got was the recorded message. What's going on?'

'I was so upset I didn't notice the phone was off . . . '

I could hear her crying quietly.

'Annie. I'm so sorry. How are you managing? What can I do?'

'Don't worry. Dad. Oh, Dad . . . Why does it have to be like this? I can't stand it. There's no one here I can talk to now Lucien's gone.'

'Listen Annie. I have to see you. You can't stay there alone. We have to meet.'

'Where are you Dad?'

'Never mind about that. I'll call you again tonight, OK? I need to make some arrangements. Please don't worry. Everything is going to be all right again. I'll take care of you from now on.'

I spent most of the day on the outside terrace of the hotel, looking at the river, and thinking about what to do next. This was perhaps the only time I had really sat down to think about my life since I was a teenager. I realised that everything I had done was a lie. I had spent my life pretending to be someone I was not, pretending to have feelings I did not have, pretending to believe things I did not really believe. My whole life had been built around pretending, around lying to other people. I had created a web of lies around myself so that no one could see who I really was. But worse, that web was now so thick and tight that I could not get out of it. I realised that lying to yourself is much worse than lying to other people.

But why? I thought back as far as I could. It probably all began with my parents' death in that terrible car accident. I was only seven years old. I had pretended to myself that they were still alive. For months I would talk to them in bed at night, pretending they were downstairs in my aunt's house, pretending that I would see them the next morning, that I only had to call them and they would come. And in the daytime, I would pretend to be brave, pretend that I could live without my parents, that I did not need them, pretend that I wasn't crying. And I pretended to like living with my aunt and her stupid husband, Uncle Len. I pretended to like playing cricket with him, and going on those long, boring Sunday afternoon walks.

And so it went on. Through my years at school and university, I was always pretending to be someone else. It was hardly surprising that I had become a spy. It was the perfect job for a professional pretender. I was paid for something which came naturally to me. It was never any effort for me to pretend to be a diplomat, a businessman, even a university professor.

After I met Francoise my wife, it was easy to pretend to love her, to give her all the things that were expected of a husband. And with a daughter, Annie, it was easy to play the role of the loving father. I would sometimes stand outside myself and think how well I was playing the part. And all the time that I was lying to them, I was also lying to myself.

Was I still pretending now? Was my concern for Annie a pretence too? I hoped it was not. I had to untangle the web of lies my life had become. It would not be easy. Annie was my last chance to change the pattern of my life, to discover who I really was.

I called Annie that evening. We arranged to meet at the railway station in Marseille in three days' time.

Chapter 23 *A New Life?*

I had plenty of time to reach Marseille, so I drove slowly, taking minor roads all the way. It was also safer like that, in case someone was following me. But I did not notice anyone. In the small hotels where I stopped, there was never anyone acting strangely, or asking too many questions. I began to feel more relaxed.

At lunchtime on the third day, I stood at St Charles station in Marseille, waiting for the Toulouse train to arrive. I felt happy and optimistic. Everything would be all right. Things would work out. I would take Annie away to a place where we would both be safe. A new life was possible. Yes, it was!

As Annie walked towards me, I could see that she was tired. Her face was pale and had a lifeless expression. I took her case and we walked slowly to the car park. She had very little to say. She seemed locked inside herself. I tried to comfort her but it was no good. When we got into the car she began to cry, tears running down her cheeks. She still said nothing. My optimistic feelings started to disappear.

I decided to drive to Aix-en-Provence and spend the night there. In the morning we would start our journey back to Sauvelagarde. We had a quiet supper. Annie still said very little, and ate less. I was beginning to feel seriously worried about her. We went to bed early.

The next day, she seemed better. She even managed a smile at breakfast. We went for a walk in the town and I talked to her about my plans. I told her that I would have to return to Sauvelagarde to get the CDs. After that we would decide on a safe place for us to live, a place where she could have her baby, where a new life could begin.

The next day we left and headed west. We drove slowly, and stopped to walk or visit places every day. I wanted to give her time to get used to me again. And every day, I felt closer to my daughter. It was as if I had never really known her before. I told her about my earlier life, about my adventures as a spy, about my failures, my mistakes, all the things I wished I'd done differently. I even told her about Nina's murder in London, and about the fire and shootings at Burstead Hall. I told her about Bert and about Peter and the whole Berlin story. I told her about the crimes of Strang and Sir Clive.

She told me about her life after I had 'disappeared' in San Cristobal. Though I had seen her a few times, she'd always kept her life to herself. She had met Lucien at the university in Toulouse. He was planning to be an engineer. They had lived together for six months. She told me about their final argument and her anger when he left her. I could hardly believe that my 'little girl' had been through all this pain and suffering. She was now a grown woman – certainly no longer a little girl.

There were times when she went completely silent. And others where she would suddenly burst into tears. I had never been much good at giving comfort to people. I never knew what to say. I tried to tell her about how I had felt when her mother and I had split up. I told her that things would get better as time passed. But I knew, even as I spoke the words, that some things never get better.

Sometimes she would explode in anger at what Lucien had done to her. 'Why me? It's so unfair. I loved him more than anyone. Why has he done this to me? I wanted his child. I wanted us to be together. Now what do I do for the rest of my life – without him? Don't you understand?'

I tried again to calm her down but it was no use. Her anger would eventually die down. When she was calmer, I would try to reason with her.

'Annie, I'm sorry about Lucien. Maybe it's better like this. Better that you should see him for what he is now, not in ten years' time.'

We talked about what to do next. I had definitely decided that after I had got the CDs, we would leave France for good. I would leave first, to find a safe place to live. She would leave later to join me. She seemed to accept this idea.

Chapter 24　*Full Circle*

A week after we left Aix-en-Provence, we were only about twenty kilometres from Sauvelagarde, almost back where I had started just a few weeks earlier. We stopped at a small restaurant on the river. It was a sunny late autumn day and we ate lunch on the terrace overlooking the bridge. Across the river, the leaves on the trees were starting to turn yellow. Autumn was coming. We were the only customers. We started to talk about the CDs. I knew I had to get them soon.

'Won't they be watching the house?' said Annie.

'Not necessarily. I don't think we've been followed. And no one will expect me to go back there. It's the last place I'd go if I had any sense. After all, they don't know I left the CDs there. But I'll be careful.'

'So how do you plan to get into the house without being seen?' asked Annie.

'I'll drive to a place above the village. It's a ruined farmhouse called le Puech. I can hide the car there. There's a steep path down through the woods. No one uses it, especially at this time of the year. I'll go down and look around to see if there are any signs of unusual activity, or any strangers about. Most of the holiday people have gone home. There are only three houses that are occupied all year round, so it's easy to notice anything unusual going on. I'll drive up there tomorrow afternoon. I'll wait till it's dark, then I'll go down to the house. If I'm careful, no one will see me. I want to say goodbye to the house, too. I'll never be able to come back.'

'But what about me? Can't I help you ?' asked Annie.

'No, Annie. It's better if you stay here. I shan't stay there long. I'll be back the same evening.'

'I don't want to be here on my own,' she said. 'I'd feel better if I was with you. You might need me.'

'Sorry, Annie. I said no, and I mean it.'

We went for a walk in the woods that afternoon. I felt closer to Annie than ever. My optimism had come back. I felt sure things were going to be all right.

That evening we were again the only guests for dinner. 'It's so nice to be eating together again,' I said.

'Yes, Dad. But it could be the last time, I suppose.'

'What do you mean, "the last"? This is the start, Annie. Our new start.'

'Maybe . . .' she replied. 'But what if something goes wrong tomorrow?'

'Nothing will go wrong. Don't be silly,' I told her.

'But, apart from that, I've been thinking, Dad . . .'

'What about?'

'Look, Dad. It's difficult for me to explain. You've been great to me these last few days. I feel as if I've got to know you properly for the first time. But . . .'

'But? But what?'

'Well, I don't think that I can go along with your plan. You've made up your mind to go off and find somewhere safe for us both to live. It's what you've decided is best for both of us. But I don't want to go anywhere else. I live here. I'm French now. I love Toulouse. I don't want to go and live on an island or wherever. I want to go on living here. And I haven't got over Lucien yet, either. I need time to get used to living without him. And I know that the best place to do that is Toulouse. That's where I live. Where I feel at home. I'm sorry, Dad, but I can't do what you want. We are two different people now. I'm not your little girl any more. I love you, and I know you love me too. But that doesn't mean we have to live together. I need my own space, Dad.'

'But you'll be in danger, Annie.'

'I don't think so, Dad. I don't know anything worth knowing. They'll soon find that out. And I won't know where you are, because you mustn't tell me.'

'But Annie, this was our chance. Everything will work out, believe me. It's the only way we can be together . . .'

'Dad, I'm sorry. You mean that it was your last chance. It's not mine. You mustn't try to live my life for me. And you can be sure that things will change for you, too. What you have been planning in your mind is just a dream. I know it hurts you now but believe me, it wouldn't work. And what about my child? Do you think I want to have to move every time you think we are being followed? And you know they will never stop looking for you, don't you?'

'But how will you manage, Annie? I mean . . .'

'Dad, I managed before, remember? Before you decided to become the world's greatest father . . . Don't worry about me. Worry about yourself. Find yourself a safe place to live. Then maybe we can think about how to meet again.'

We argued backwards and forwards for the whole evening. Nothing I said could make her change her mind. It was late when we went to bed. I slept badly.

Chapter 25   *Endgame*

I got up at four o'clock and decided to go to the house straight away, before it got light. I dressed quickly and left the hotel quietly. It was five o'clock when I drove into the farmyard at le Puech. The windows of the farmhouse were broken and the farmyard was overgrown with weeds and tall grass. It was still dark. The path from the farm ran down steeply through the trees and bushes, towards the village. It was a rocky path, formerly used by shepherds to bring the sheep down from the high fields to the village. Now it was unused and overgrown with bushes. I slowly made my way down the path, taking care not to make a noise. Every few minutes I stopped to listen. There was nothing – just the wind in the leaves and the sound of the river far below. Just before the village, I stopped at a place overlooking the square. The village was in darkness. No one was around. I went down the path to the edge of the village and took one of the old roads towards my own house. There was still no sign of anything unusual. From the cover of some bushes I could now see the dark shape of my own house. I made my way to the door of the tunnel under the road, opened it, and went in.

The house was just as I had left it. I went up into the kitchen and opened the table drawer. The brown envelope with the CDs was there. I put it carefully away in my rucksack and went back down to the tunnel and out of the house.

My mind was still upside-down from the argument with Annie. I wanted to think clearly, to find a solution that she could accept, to find the right words to make her change her mind. I decided to take a quick walk down to the river. It would help to clear my head. There was no danger now. I had seen no one. It would be my last chance to see the river I love so much. I would never come back here. I walked quickly down the path towards the river. It was beginning to get light – the grey light that comes just before dawn.

An Underground Station in London

It is the evening rush hour at a busy London underground station. The name of the station on the wall is Liverpool Street, on the Central Line. The platform is very crowded. People push against each other as they prepare to get on the overcrowded tube. Halfway down the platform a man in a grey suit is looking nervously about him. He is holding an old black briefcase and a newspaper. A train comes into the station. Suddenly there is a lot of shouting and a woman screams. Something has happened. Someone has fallen in front of the train. The man in the grey suit is dead. He must have lost his balance on the crowded platform. It seems to be an awful accident.

The Valley

It is early morning in October. The scene is a valley in south-western France. The river runs slowly between steep wooded slopes. A man is sitting on a flat rock by a river. Mist is rising from the river and fills the valley. Autumn leaves float on the surface of the river. It is quiet – there is only the noise of the water running by the mill lower down. The man is deep in thought. He sits absolutely still, like a stone statue. Another man, dressed in black, is watching him from the woods above the river. He raises a rifle and takes careful aim. He pulls the trigger slowly, deliberately. The man on the rock suddenly falls forward into the river. He floats face down in the water. The slow current of the river carries away a steady flow of blood from a wound in his head. Another man appears. He walks forward and watches the body slowly float away. The man with the rifle joins him. Then they both walk away into the mist. A few minutes later the sound of a powerful motorbike echoes along the valley.

A Drug Overdose at Headquarters

An elegantly-dressed man is sitting at a large desk in an office overlooking the River Thames. It is late afternoon. Outside the November rain is falling. On his desk there is an evening newspaper with large headlines. The man picks up a pen and writes a short note. When he has finished, he gets up, with great difficulty. He uses two walking sticks to help him walk to the window. He stands for a moment, taking a last look at the river below, then he closes the blinds. He goes back to sit at the desk, opens a bottle of pills, pours them into his hand and swallows them all with a glass of water. Within minutes his head drops forward on to the desk. He does not move. His head partly covers the newspaper headline: MI6 CHIEF ACCUSED.

Cambridge English Readers

Look out for these other titles in the series:

Level 5

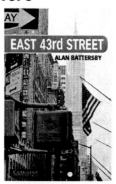

East 43rd Street
by Alan Battersby

New York, six days before Christmas. Nathan Marley is relaxing in McFadden's Bar. A woman walks in and out of the bar and Marley follows her. Christmas is about to become a lot more exciting for Marley.

Emergency Murder
by Janet McGiffin

When the wife of a surgeon dies suddenly in a hospital in Milwaukee, USA, Dr Maxine Cassidy suspects murder. When someone tries to kill her, she wonders which of her colleagues she can trust.

Dolphin Music
by Antoinette Moses

The year is 2051. CONTROL, the government of Europe, keeps everyone happy in a virtual reality. This is a world where wonderful music made by dolphins gives everyone pleasure. When Saul Grant discovers the truth, the illusion is shattered and he sets out to free the dolphins.

The Sugar Glider
by Rod Neilsen

Pilot Don Radcliffe returns to Australia hoping to spend more time with his daughter, Judy. But a routine cargo flight turns into tragedy when the plane crashes, killing the co-pilot. Dan and Judy's chances of survival seem slim.